Questions from a
Single Heart

Linda~
I pray this
book will encourage
you.   Laura A. Smith
Psalm 119:10

Questions from a
Single Heart

A New

Perspective on

Singleness and a

Deeper Understanding

of God's Purpose for

Your Life

Laura A. Smith

WinePressPublishing
Your Book, Defined. Since 1991.

WinePress Publishing (PO Box 428, Enumclaw, WA 98022) functions only as book publisher. As such, the ultimate design, content, editorial accuracy, and views expressed or implied in this work are those of the author.

Unless otherwise noted, all Scriptures are taken from the *New King James Version*®. Copyright © 1982 by Thomas Nelson, Inc. Used by permission. All rights reserved.

ISBN 13: 978-1-4141-1735-5
ISBN 10: 1-4141-1735-3
Library of Congress Catalog Card Number: 2010902676

Contents

Introduction: Why Write This Book?

THE POPULATION OF singles is increasing, yet singlehood remains a lonely place for many. As a single woman, I see an ever-growing need for encouragement for single people. Some of the books written on this topic have not resonated with me. Instead, they've left me feeling depressed and a bit like a failure because I haven't been able to conquer every feeling of disappointment in my single situation. The reality is that no person, no matter what the circumstances, will ever defeat every problem area in his or her life. Realizing this while at the same time maintaining a healthy, joyful attitude, does lead to a fulfilled and happy life.

So what makes this book different? I write from a place of experience. I have lived the single life, and what you'll read in these pages is not hearsay. I've struggled through the discouragement and come through to the other side with true victory.

Recently I listened in a church service while a college student sang about the many difficulties of life, the trials, and the hard times. He sang about how he wouldn't change any of them because through it all he saw that God was good. My very unspiritual thought at the moment was, *Kid, when you're my age and you've had some loved ones die; been so poor you cancelled your cell phone, cable, and the newspaper so you could afford groceries; or your health has failed you for a time, then you'll be qualified to sing that song.* From my point of view, he hadn't lived through any of the circumstances he was singing about, and therefore, his words didn't seem credible to me.

I am now thirty-eight years old, not an old person by any means, but never having been married, I qualify as an experienced single person. I have cried from loneliness at times, and I have experienced God's incredible comfort. When everything is going well or one is in a fun relationship, it's easy to pontificate on God's goodness and how one has learned to depend on God. The hard times of deep loneliness are when one's dependence on God is truly tested. Because I have struggled through these issues, I can offer insight to help the single person overcome these problem areas. And I pray that I will write this with the passion and lack of self-righteousness needed to touch others.

As I set out on this writing journey, I am in the trenches of singleness. I'm not in a boyfriend/girlfriend relationship right now, and I'm not married. I am a single person. Yet I do find over and over that God is good. I can depend on Him, and the peace He gives is boundless. Even in the midst of sad moments, I can smile and know I'm worth more to God than I could be to any person on earth. I've dug into Scripture, and I feel more positive about the single situation than I ever have previously. Not only am I now better equipped to deal with singleness, but I also have a renewed hope that God has a plan for my life, whether it is with or without a husband—and I am not denying the possibility that my future may yet include a spouse. I also know when that college kid is thirty-eight, fifty-eight, or even eighty-eight, he will have suffered through many more of life's experiences and will still be able to sing that God is good.

This book has a dual purpose. Not only will I address the growing population of single adults, but also I want to help married people better understand and assist single people. The struggle to refrain from bitterness can leave the single person smiling and cheering on the outside when they feel a little bit like dying on the inside. The alternative is to actually let bitterness take over, and what a disaster that is! The temptation is strong, however, and constantly before single people.

Once I had an office job where I sat directly across from the open break room, and every day someone brought in tempting pastries, cookies, or donuts. Each day I would resolve *not* to eat those enticing, fattening foods; but the temptation was constantly before me. I could smell the food and see others eating it. It was in front of my eyes all day long. Singles often feel the same way about what is in front of them. They see happy couples leaving church together, children running to their mothers, and families planning their annual vacations. Faced with looking at those fantastic-appearing relationships, the temptation is strong to feel sad and left out.

Years ago I found the only way to combat those pastry temptations was to replace the bad temptation with something good—something I actually wanted to eat or do that was healthy for me. In this book, you will find a substitution to bitterness and sadness, and you'll be happy to discover that the alternative in your single life is much better than a diet of carrot sticks and celery. Each single person can lead a wonderful life full of meaning and joy.

Because married people play a role in a single person's life, this book is for them to read too. Unlike their married counterparts, single people don't have someone to share their struggles with or to talk to when someone has said something mean. Singles often sit alone at church. Many do not have children who run to them for kisses and hugs. And every year that much-needed vacation looms and they throw out the all-too-familiar prayer: *Please, God, let me find someone fun to visit or something great to do for a vacation this year. Please don't let me have to go by myself.*

If you're married, at this point you might be saying, "Umm, do these single people not realize married people fight and have their challenges too? Do they forget about the poopy diapers and the tight budgets that sometimes mean no vacation at all?" Perhaps at times we do forget that the grass is not always greener on the other side, but I want us to realize it isn't married versus single. God put each of us here to serve a purpose, serve each other, and glorify Him.

My final reason for writing this book is the fresh discovery of an inspirational single person in the Bible. All of my adult life I've wished for a biblical example of a single woman, someone I could relate to. I wanted to see how a Bible character handled the challenges of being single, but such a woman didn't seem to exist. Recently, I was reading my Bible, and I found that person. She has been right there all of the time. How could I have missed her all of these years? As I excitedly began to discover and share with my friends the parallels of this woman's life to mine as a single person, they unanimously agreed with me that they'd never thought of her this way before either, but she fits the example we've all been wanting. The more I read about this amazing woman, the more I realized that she simply applied God's promises and commands to her life. That is how she lived as a single woman, and God did bless her. Furthermore, she stood strong. She did not give in to wrong choices. Throughout these pages, I will parallel this single woman's life with life lessons for singles of today.

My prayer is that as you read the following pages, issues which cause singles to struggle will be practically and biblically addressed. I pray this book will be uplifting and fun for you to read while strengthening your resolve to live as a godly single person.

CHAPTER 1

Why Must I Be Alone?

*R*UTH SIGHED HEAVILY *and looked sideways at her mother-in-law, Naomi. She was worried about her. They both had suffered so much loss, but now Naomi was letting it consume her. Ruth's heart was heavy with her own loss, and her heart ached with love and compassion for Naomi.*

Ruth closed her eyes tightly for just a moment and pictured herself several years earlier. She had been so young when she had met Naomi and her two sons. Initially, she'd been impressed with the peace Naomi possessed. Even though Naomi had already experienced significant sorrow, she had a quality that drew Ruth to her.

Naomi and her husband, Elimelech, had left their homeland because of a famine in the land. Moab,

Ruth's country, was experiencing prosperity at the time, and so it had seemed like a good place for Naomi and Elimelech to come and live with their two sons, both of whom had been weak and sickly from birth. Moab was a long way from Bethlehem, though, where Naomi had lived her whole life. There would be no visiting back and forth; Bethlehem was on the other side of the Salt Sea and so far, far away.

Not long after that, Elimelech died suddenly, and Naomi was left alone with just her two sons. That's when Ruth met the family, and Naomi began to tell Ruth about her God. This God was so completely different than the gods Ruth had grown up worshiping. Naomi spoke of Him in a personal way, as if her God knew her individually.

At first Ruth was simply intrigued, but the more she heard, the more she desired to know this God. She had brought her friend Orpah to meet Naomi, and together they listened while Naomi described a God who had created the world and yet still concerned Himself with the daily activities of her own life.

One day Naomi quoted a beautiful promise about God gathering His children under His wings. That day Ruth realized she must forsake the cold, helpless gods she'd worshipped her entire life. These gods she had been brought up to revere were made out of wood and stone by mere men. Her gods did not care about her well-being. In fact, Ruth had spent most of her time worrying about angering her gods or doing anything that would displease them. This God Naomi served actually had created her and the world in which she lived. He was intimately involved in the lives of those who worshipped Him.

Both Ruth and Orpah had come to the age of marriage, and with their new knowledge of God, it had made sense to marry someone who shared their faith. Ruth married Naomi's son Mahlon, and Orpah married the other son, Chilion.

For years they had lived together, growing stronger in their faith in God. Sometimes it was hard to understand why God did not bless either Ruth or Orpah with a child, but Ruth's faith in God's goodness and provision for her remained strong. Then tragedy struck, and then it struck again. First Mahlon died, and then Chilion died—one right after the other. The grief was almost unbearable, and perhaps because of the grief, Naomi began to long for the land of her birth. The famine in Bethlehem was long past, and so the three women decided to make the journey to Naomi's homeland.

They had reached the border of Moab the previous night, and Naomi had begun to urge both Ruth and Orpah to return to their mothers. "Stay in Moab," she said over and over. "Find new husbands for yourselves in Moab." Perhaps Naomi knew all too well how difficult it was to be a foreign woman in a strange *land. Besides, what could she offer these two women? She had no more sons for them.*

After much pleading and arguing, Orpah had decided to return home. Ruth and Naomi had kissed Orpah goodbye that morning, and Naomi had continued to weep throughout the day as if her very heart had been torn out of her.

Ruth looked again at Naomi, and their eyes connected. Naomi began to urge Ruth again to go back home. Ruth knew if she left Naomi, her mother-in-law would die of a broken heart. She stopped walking and turned towards Naomi; taking her wrinkled hands in her own and speaking softly she said, "Naomi, I'm not going to leave you. I will go where you go and live where you live. Your God is my God now."

Naomi put her arms around Ruth, and the two women clung to each other for a long time. Ruth prayed silently, God, help me to be strong. Help me to be strong for Naomi right now. We've both lost so much.

A good friend of mine recently asked me, "Laura, are you baffled that we're still single?" I hadn't really connected the word *baffled* to my situation, but as I thought about it, yes, I had to admit that I was a little baffled. Both she and I are relatively attractive people with what I'd like to believe are nice personalities. We've both worked hard and have good jobs. So why are we still single?

For as long as I can remember, all I ever wanted to do was grow up, get married, and have a family of my own. When I was about nine years old, my siblings and I went to a school in Soap Lake, a little town plopped down in the middle of the dry deserts of Eastern Washington. The only claim to fame for the town is a lake that supposedly has healing powers due to the minerals that have washed down into it from the surrounding basalt cliffs, leaving the lake with a soapy substance that is hard to wash off after you go swimming in it.

Near our school was a little, run-down house where a hermit allegedly lived. I never would have walked by that house by myself, but with an older sibling or friend by my side, I would always slow my steps and stare intently at the heavily-blinded windows and unkempt yard, hoping for a glimpse of the hermit. I was fascinated by the notion that someone would lock himself away from all humanity. Honestly, I couldn't imagine that kind of solitude.

One day my older brother was teasing me merci-lessly. In anger and frustration, I announced that when I grew up I was going to move into the hills and live as a hermit. No one would be able to tease me then. Oh, if only I'd known how much worse I'd just made my situation. Even my own mother began to laugh. She said, "You as a hermit? You can't even sit and read a book by yourself. You have to go find someone to be near you all the time."

To this day, my siblings will occasionally tease me about my proclamation that I would grow up to be a hermit. It was just so ridiculous. I was the last candidate in the world for being a hermit.

So, yes, I have been baffled as to why I'm still single. I have asked from time to time, *Why me, God? Why out of all the people in the world do you choose me to be a single person?* I don't like being alone. I go to the grocery store sometimes just so I'll run into people. I have even answered the phone when I knew it was going to be a telemarketer because I wanted human contact. But this is an area of my life I've had to turn over to God. He knows me and my personality and has decided for some reason to let me remain single. Scripture tells us, "'For My thoughts are not your thoughts, Nor are your ways My ways,' says the LORD" (Isa. 55:8).

God Has a Plan

This book is not about why you are single. God is the only one who knows why, and trying to figure it out is a poor use of our energy. Perhaps God wants you to draw closer to Him, or perhaps you are an important player in God's plan for the world. You cannot see or even comprehend the complicated plan God has in mind, and your obedience to Him means more than you'll ever be able to understand on this earth.

No matter what situations are presented to you in life, there will always be an opportunity to say, "Why me?" Ruth so easily could have fallen into that mindset. She could have said, "Why did my husband die? Why don't I have any children? Why does Naomi insist we go to Bethlehem and then cry when Orpah wants to go home?" However, we never see any of that in Ruth's life. Instead, she put her faith in God and moved forward. By the end of this book, you will understand that the story of Ruth is so much more than a love story. The role God had her play is vitally important to you and to me.

Ruth did something else that is important. She stood firmly in her faith in God. Returning to Moab and finding an unsaved husband would have been so easy. Even Naomi encouraged her to do this. Recklessly, she told Ruth to return to the gods of Moab. Sadly, I also have experienced older, and who should have been wiser, Christians who have tried to persuade me to make compromises in my relationships that would have dishonored

God. Some of the words they've used to describe me have hurt deeply, such as, "You're too picky and choosey." At times those unfair statements have caused me to question my resolve to stay at the center of God's will for my life. There may be times when you will have to take a firm stand and stand firmly alone. Know that God has not forgotten your situation. Ruth too had to stand all alone.

Can you trust a God who is infinitely wiser than you to take control of your life? Can you believe He has something important for you (yes, you) to do? Take hold of the thought that your obedience to God means everything.

CHAPTER 2

Why Do Lawn Mowers Make Me Cry?

*R*UTH WAS BEGINNING *to feel excited. Naomi had been telling her for two days now that they were close, very close to Bethlehem. Ruth brushed her hand nervously across her forehead and scanned the horizon. Were her eyes deceiving her or were they actually finally coming to Bethlehem? Naomi reached over and grasped Ruth's hand. "We're here," she whispered. "We're finally home."*

As the two women made their way into the city, Ruth was thrilled as the entire town seemed to embrace Naomi. Surely being with her own people would help Naomi's heartaches heal, but what was Naomi telling her friends? She was telling them not to call her Naomi any longer. "Call me Mara, because my life is full of bitterness," she said. "I went away from you with a husband and two sons. I come back to you empty. God has afflicted me."

Naomi's words "I've come back empty" stung. Both she and Naomi had lost so much, but Ruth had clung to the fact that they had each other. Ruth blinked back the tears that threatened to spill out of her eyes and sucked a shaky breath of air past her aching heart and into her lungs. She felt as if her heart were being crushed under a heavy weight. Am I nothing at all to her? *Ruth let the thought linger for only a moment before she considered the greater insult Naomi had made towards God. If God truly had afflicted her, would He have allowed Naomi to return to Bethlehem, where friends welcomed her with open arms?*

Ruth pushed thoughts of self-pity aside. I must, I will help Naomi remember that the great God we serve would never abandon us.

The sun warmed the back of my neck as I carefully examined the socket wrench. I was trying to remember how one goes about reversing the direction so that I could loosen the spark plug instead of tightening it more. After several attempts at twisting and turning, I finally remembered that I needed to push in the little button and turn at the same time. By now my knees were starting to hurt from kneeling on asphalt, so I plopped down and sat in my driveway. Looking at the dirty old spark plug, I tried to guess which socket would be the right size. After a few tries, I felt the socket slip over the spark plug and got the resistance I needed. I began to feel excitement as it came loose and then fell out. With glee, I changed the direction of my wrench and placed the new plug into my lawn mower. I jumped up and ran back into the garage for a screwdriver. I wasn't sure what kind of filter I was removing, but dad had told me I could clean it with gasoline and it'd be as good as new. I checked the oil level, filled up the tank with gasoline, gave it a few primer spritzes, and then held my breath while I yanked the starter rope. On the second yank, my little, old lawn mower that had sat in a damp shed all winter burst to life. You would have thought I'd just repaired a fighter jet! Only those who know me best could know what a victory this was. As I happily pushed the mower around the yard, I allowed my memories to wander back several years.

I was only twenty-four years old when I bought the house with a big lawn; and I had been relieved when I spotted the rusty, old lawn mower in the shed. Here was an expense I could avoid for awhile. Now I owned a house and a lawn mower.

That lawn mower caused me nothing but grief. It did run, but it had a temperament all its own. The lawn mower never started with less than twenty or thirty pulls, and if it didn't start by the thirtieth pull, I might as well just put it back in the shed and wait until the next day. I knew I could splash starter fluid into it with reckless abandon and pull until I'd yanked my arm off. It simply would not start if it wasn't in the mood to start. Nine times out of ten, I would get it started, but then I'd have to mow like mad because it only had about forty minutes of mowing time in it. Once it died, it absolutely would not start again on the same day. Cursed with a one-track mind, if I'd decided it was time to mow my lawn, anything that got in my way could thrust me into the depths of despair. You can only imagine how defeated I felt when I had to leave a section in the middle of my backyard un-mowed because the lawn mower died eight minutes before I was finished.

After an entire summer of partially-mowed lawns, I finally came to the realization that spending money on a new mower would be worth a few weeks of frugality in other areas. Dad told me I couldn't go wrong as long as I bought something with a Briggs and Stratton engine. When I arrived at the hardware store, it seemed it might be my lucky day. The salesman told me he had a reconditioned mower. "It really isn't used," he stated. "It's been returned, but we checked it completely over, and it's perfect. We've taken fifty dollars off the original price."

Wow! What great news for me. "I'll take it," I said with a smile. "Do you think someone could help me load it into the trunk of my car?" The salesman was more than accommodating.

I got home with the thing, and in a death-defying move, I got it out of the trunk of the car all by myself. It was about eight PM, so if I hurried, I could get my grass mowed before the sun went down. The gas tank was already partially full, but I topped it off and yanked on the starter rope. That lawn mower coughed and sputtered its way to life, and with the roar of the engine came billowing clouds of black smoke. Suddenly the cul-de-sac seemed to be full of neighbors, and one of them yelled, "Hey, Laura, it's not the Fourth of July!"

I quickly killed the engine and scooted into my garage. I felt so embarrassed. I should have found someone to help me load it back into my car, but instead, I somehow managed to get it back into the trunk on my own. I went and sat on my couch and cried before going back to the hardware store.

At the hardware store, the salesman took a look at it and said, "Hmmm, looks like someone put oil in the gas tank. Sometimes the guys that go over these returns aren't as thorough as we'd like them to be. Sorry about that." He sold me a new lawn mower for full price, and I drove back home. By now it was pitch black, and I knew I couldn't mow the lawn. I could almost hear the stalks of grass swishing together in the wind, but surely tomorrow would be a better day.

The next day I once again manhandled the mower out of the trunk and then carefully added the gasoline. I went around the yard picking up sticks and moving hoses and other things out of the way. At last, I could finally get this messy yard back into shape. I leaned forward, grasped the pull cord, and gave a tug. The starter cord pulled out, but the engine did not burst to life. Instead, as I released the rope, it snarled and tangled up inside the starter cage. I reached down to tug it again, but it was stuck fast in its knotted mess. I began to cry. I looked at my messy lawn and at my scraped up arms, where I'd hurt myself getting the lawn mower in and out of the car. I looked at my rusty old mower now pushed off to the side, and I began to sob. I walked into my kitchen, picked up the phone, dialed my mother, and between gasps and sobs told her, "This is why I need a husband."

Everyone laughs when I tell that story now, but at the time, I was so frustrated and was feeling alone. I wanted to give up on this game of trying to take care of myself. I had started down the road of self-pity.

Choose Your Attitude

Self-pity is a very dangerous indulgence. I never have felt better after a pity party—not even once. Through the years I've had quite a few pity parties for myself, and I never can get anyone else to come to them. Do you know why? It's because nobody likes being around a whiner. Oh so slowly, I began to learn to deal with the frustrations of being unable to do things by myself. Sometimes I had to swallow my pride and ask for help; sometimes I had to put off doing things that I really, really wanted to get done right that moment.

Gradually, I began to remember to apply biblical principles instead of crying. The results are so much better. The following steps are ones I now often take when I'm presented with opposition to my goals.

1. Try to think of every reason to be thankful in the particular situation in which you find yourself. "Giving thanks always for all things to God the Father in the name of our Lord Jesus Christ" (Eph. 5:20). For instance, with the lawn mower, I would thank God that:

15

a. I have a lawn to mow. And not only do I have a lawn, but I also have a home that goes with it. In India, houses for entire towns are made of cardboard.

b. I have arms that can get scraped. How thankful I am for my two strong arms. I know someone whose arms did not develop in the womb. He would be thankful for scraped up arms.

c. I have a car in which I can *again* drive to the store. That's right, my lawnmower may not be running, but my car is.

Everyone's list is different. You may not have as much to be materially thankful for, but you have something for which you can be thankful. If you are ill, have you ever wondered what it would be like to have the same illness in a third world country? In the United States you have access to the greatest healthcare in the world.

Sometimes we cannot make sense of why God would ask us to give thanks in all things, but we are human and cannot see all that God sees. I love the book *The Hiding Place*. During their time in a concentration camp, Corrie and Betsie Ten Boom found themselves in a barrack that was infested with lice. If ever anyone had a reason to indulge in self-pity, the Ten Boom women had been given that reason. Instead, Betsie insisted that they thank God for the lice. Corrie resisted; surely God did not intend for them to be thankful for lice. But Betsie reminded her that the Bible says in *everything* give thanks. Grudgingly, Corrie thanked God for the lice. Later, she and Betsie had uncensored access to share God's love with the other women in their living quarters because the guards wouldn't come close to them because of the lice. Giving thanks for lice didn't make sense from a human perspective, but God could see the big picture.

2. Do something fun instead of working. All of that thankfulness usually puts me into a better frame of mind. I'm not sure I can attach a biblical principle to this and the following suggestion, but they are a direct result of an adjusted attitude. I figure if that many things went wrong, I am entitled to skip doing something productive for one evening.

3. Remember, almost everything eventually makes a good story. People have told me repeatedly that I have great stories. I really don't think my life is that unusual, but I do think I look at things a bit differently. I'm always on the lookout for the next great story, and if it means I'll have a few dreadful moments in order for the story to

materialize, it'll be worth it when everyone is laughing about Laura's latest predicament.

Do these suggestions seem trite and obvious? They probably do. Doing what is right and good is typically pretty simple. But remember, how you deal with the stuff of life is dependent on your attitude.

We've been reading the story of my favorite, and what I believe is the greatest, biblical example of a single woman. She lived how God wanted her to live. Let's, for a moment, consider Ruth and her situation. (By the way, this story has a nice romantic ending, so you really do need to keep reading to the end of the book.)

Ruth's husband died, and she was left to take care of Naomi, who, by her own admission, was bitter because her husband and both of her sons had died, leaving her with two daughters-in-law (one of whom had left her) and no grandchildren. She told her friends to no longer call her Naomi but to call her bitterness. Can you imagine deciding to stay with someone who goes around saying, "Just call me bitterness"? Yet Ruth decided to do just that. She moved with her mother-in-law to Bethlehem. She left her friends, family, and country to stay with her mother-in-law because she believed it was the right thing to do.

I've often wondered if Naomi really was bitter or just being dramatic when she told her friends to call her bitterness and that God had afflicted her. I actually like Naomi, even though you're probably thinking by now that I'm hard on her. Perhaps I like her because her life reminds me that God blesses us in spite of ourselves. Let's face it, most of us have behaved more like Naomi than Ruth at some point in our lives. The Bible tells us that Ruth loved Naomi, so initially there must have been something in Naomi that drew Ruth to her. However, at this time, Naomi was not being a good example.

Unfortunately, what comes out of our mouths generally starts in our hearts. Every indication is that Naomi did not stay bitter. Yet she was bitter for a time, and it is recorded for every human being to read. Be cautious not to let bitterness take hold in your life. Bitterness is likened to a root in the Bible: "...lest any root of bitterness springing up cause trouble, and by this many become defiled" (Heb. 12:15). Have you ever tried to get rid of a root to a tree or weed? Those crazy little things grow out and wrap around sticks and rocks. If the whole thing doesn't get taken out, it can start growing again, and then the whole surgery of removing it has to be repeated. Don't let it get started in the first place, and if it does begin to grow, rip it out quickly. Never allow yourself to think or say things like, *God has forgotten me*, or *He doesn't care about me.*

Ruth's situation was no better than Naomi's. In fact, it may have been worse. Both Naomi and Ruth were widows. Both Naomi and Ruth were childless. Maybe Ruth wondered if she was even capable of having children. She'd been married to Mahlon for ten years without having a child. Ruth had the additional sorrow of being far from home and family. Naomi had Ruth to care for her in her old age. Ruth didn't have anyone who would be able to care for her when she grew old. So what really made the difference between these two women? Attitude made all the difference. Naomi chose bitterness, and Ruth chose to accept her situation and work towards making it better.

With the possibility of making my great-grandmothers roll over in their graves, I'm going to describe two of them to you. Both women were Christians, but their lives were drastically different, both in situation and happiness.

My great-grandmother Hirschel had a relatively easy and normal life. Of course, it wasn't completely trial-free. No person's life ever is. But in general, her life was comfortable and free of pain. Her husband was kind and well respected. She was not wealthy, but she never lacked for necessities or the comforts of life. She was one of the healthiest elderly women I've ever known.

My great-grandmother Miller, on the other hand, led a different life. When she was fifteen, she married a much older man. I do not know the circumstances of why she married so young, but this was over one hundred years ago and was not uncommon. Her husband immediately moved her far from her home and family. She had a total of eight children. My great-grandfather did not treat her well. He sometimes would get drunk and be unbearable and abusive. Often, she barely had enough food to feed the children. Then when my great-grandfather became elderly, he developed cancer, and she cared for him as he slowly died.

I'm named for one of these women, and I've always been proud to bear her name. I never knew her personally because she died when I was an infant, but every description of her has been about what a fun, happy person she always was and how everyone absolutely loved her.

I did know my other great-grandmother. I remember her being bitter and grumpy, even when I was a child. She was self-centered and complained all of the time. She was so negative that she could find the downside of a birthday party.

So which great-grandmother would you expect to be the fun, happy person? You would think that it was the one with a comfortable life, but it wasn't; it was great-grandmother Miller.

One great-grandma had a good life, but her attitude was one of bitterness and complaints. She was an unhappy person. The other great-grandma had a hard life, but her attitude was brilliant. I wish I could have known her personally. I probably would have asked her how she maintained her buoyant spirit. I suspect from what I've been told about her that she would have said, "What good would it do to complain?"

I am thankful for my great-grandmother Miller. Sometimes God puts these spiritual giants in our path to remind us of what He wants us to be. Even though her life was tough, she didn't go around feeling sorry for herself.

After all of these years, I'll still tell you my lawn mower troubles were frustrating. However, crying over my lawn mower did not change the situation. The tears did not make my mower start, and it certainly didn't find me a husband. The only thing that could have changed the situation was my own attitude.

CHAPTER 3

What's Wrong with Me?

R*UTH STRAIGHTENED UP and stretched her back. She had traveled all the way from Moab, but this was an entirely different kind of exercise. Her back was beginning to ache from stooping over. Yet gathering this grain was a way for Naomi and her to remain self-sufficient.*

Ruth and Naomi had arrived in Bethlehem at the beginning of barley harvest. Even this seemed providential to Ruth. The law of the Israelites provided for widows to go behind the harvesters and glean grain that was dropped or missed. Ruth had asked Naomi if she could go glean in the harvest fields, and Naomi had given her blessing.

As Ruth shifted the basket of grain to her left side, she caught a glimpse of a man approaching. Please,

God, let him be kind to me. He must wonder why I think I have a right as a foreigner to be in his field.

The man did not look upset, though. As he drew close, he began to speak to her. He wasn't asking her why she was there. Instead, he was telling her to continue gleaning in his fields and that she was welcome to drink water that his men drew from his own well. He wanted her to know she would be safe in his fields.

Ruth's heart was overwhelmed with thankfulness. She would not need to move from field to field, always wondering if the owner would question her right to be there. She dropped to her knees and gratefully asked the man, "Why are you being so kind to me when I am a stranger in your country?"

The man, Ruth would later learn his name was Boaz, said, "I've been told what you've done for your mother-in-law since your husband died and how you left your father and mother and the land where you were born to come and live here. May the God of Israel, under whose wings you've put your trust, reward you."

I was good at these events and could usually get people talking about themselves and then coast through with smiles and nods and questions that were appropriately spaced. Once in a while, someone would ask me about myself, and I would usually oblige them by talking a bit. That night, however, I was tired. I'd been on the road for two weeks, and they had not been fun weeks. If I could just make it through this social hour, I'd be through with my obligations. In the morning, I'd be on a plane headed for home.

I'd been chatting with one of my co-workers when her husband walked up. "Laura, I'd like you to meet my husband, Mike." After the introduction, she was instantly distracted by someone else, and I was left to make idle chat with Mike. Mike mentioned that he and his wife had just celebrated their fifth anniversary. I congratulated him and asked how they'd met. The story was a fairly interesting one, and he was pretty happy to tell it. His life and photography had been featured in a magazine article. When his future wife read the article, she was touched by his story. Since they were from relatively the same area, she contacted him. The typical road blocks ensued, but they pressed on, and ta-dah, here they were married.

This is good, I thought. *I'm making it through the evening. Soon I'll be heading home.*

Mike then asked the typical and completely acceptable questions, "What about you, Laura, are you married? Do you have children?"

I answered with my usual, "No, I'm not married, and I don't have any children, but I look forward to both." This usually ends the conversation and allows both of us to keep our dignity. But, unfortunately, for me, this is where the whole evening took a rather nasty turn.

"Really? Well, have you ever been engaged?" asked Mike.

This is not a pleasant question to be on the other end of, no matter what the answer is. I mustered a smile as my recently ended relationship flashed through my mind, "No, I have not."

"Oh," Mike replied, "so you're fussy."

I instantly felt something inside of me shrivel, and although I willed a smile to my face, I could feel my shoulders slump. "No, I'm not fussy," I responded.

"Oh, well then, what's wrong with you?"

Later, I described this moment to my sister as the feeling I expect a deer feels when it is caught in someone's headlights. I should have given myself permission to walk away, but my mind had gone numb. "There's nothing wrong with me," I replied.

"Well, something must be wrong with you. You're an attractive woman, but at least you're not as bad as my friend who is fifty-three. He's been engaged like five times but can never seem to make it to the altar."

I don't remember most of the remainder of that conversation, but it was painful, as he told me at least three more times that there must be something wrong with me.

Later, I asked myself why I hadn't just walked away. At the time I had felt it was important to protect my working relationship with his wife, and I also felt I could handle the insults. The truth was the insults hurt deeply, whether or not they were true. The one thought most singles do battle is, *What's wrong with me? Why hasn't someone chosen me (or at least someone I would choose back)?*

Be the Right Person

Have you ever considered that maybe it isn't what is wrong with you but rather what is right with you? Perhaps the choices you've made have been difficult and meant you had to give up a relationship you wanted but knew was not honoring to God. You alone had to make the decision to do what was right even if it meant following the harder path.

You may be wondering what the Ruth story at the beginning of this chapter possibly could have to do with the chapter title, What's Wrong with

Me? For Ruth, it really was more about what was right with her. Because she and Naomi needed food, Ruth went out each day to glean grain in the fields. This could not have been a fun job, but she did it because it was the right thing to do. Ruth was unique, and it made her stand out from the crowd. In fact, there was something so special about her that Boaz noticed her working and asked his workers about her situation.

When Ruth asked him why he took notice of her, he stated everyone knew what she'd done for her mother-in-law. Ruth was not single because there was something wrong with her. She could have stayed in Moab. Naomi certainly had suggested that Ruth stay in Moab and marry someone from her own country, but that would have meant marrying someone who did not believe in the one true God. That would have meant abandoning Naomi. No, Ruth was not single because there was something wrong with her. Ruth was single because she had done exactly what God wanted her to do.

Oh, I get a shiver thinking about it. Ruth had no idea what God was preparing for her. Think about what would have happened to her if she had decided to pity herself instead. Staying home each day and moping about the house with Naomi certainly could have been a temptation.

Honestly, everyone does have areas in which they can improve. We shouldn't ignore those areas either. I used to joke that every single person has at least one major thing wrong with him or her that is keeping that person from getting married. I also said that if someone would just tell me what my one major wrong thing was, I'd correct it. The truth is, we usually can self-detect the areas we need to improve. Be honest with yourself and start working on those areas.

Finally, remember that God has chosen you! God does think you are special. He thinks you are so incredibly special that if you were the only person on earth, He still would have sent His Son to die for you. The Bible tells us God was not willing for any to perish. (See 2 Peter 3:9.) You are infinitely more precious to God than you could ever be to another human being.

CHAPTER 4

Why Do I Keep Looking?

R UTH, HOW DID you collect so much grain in one day?" Naomi asked. "Someone certainly has taken special notice of you."

Ruth smiled at the incredulous look on Naomi's face as she looked at the grain Ruth had been able to collect in just one day's time. Ruth had suspected she was getting a little extra help. The workers had seemed particularly careless, almost as if they were purposefully dropping grain right in front of her.

Ruth then explained how Boaz had approached her and recommended that she glean only from his field. She also told Naomi she'd been surprised when Boaz had given her food to eat and water to drink.

"Whose field did you say you were gleaning in?"

"Some of the other women told me that the field belonged to Boaz, and it was Boaz himself who spoke to me."

Naomi's eyes began to shine as she said, "Oh, Ruth, God has not forgotten us after all. Boaz is a near relative to my deceased husband, Elimelech. Stay in his fields. Don't go anywhere else to get grain. Glean only from his fields until the end of harvest."

And so Ruth returned each day to the field of Boaz until the end of the harvest season. When all the grain had been gathered and taken to the threshing floor, Naomi gave Ruth a new set of instructions.

"Ruth, my faithful daughter, I want you to be secure with a husband. Tonight I want you to go to the threshing floor. When Boaz has eaten and gone to lie down, notice where it is he goes to sleep. After he falls asleep, go uncover his feet so he'll get cold. Lie down at his feet and wait for him to wake up from the cold. He'll understand your intentions, and he will tell you what to do."

That night, Ruth felt nervous as she approached the threshing area. These seemed like such strange instructions, but Ruth had always trusted Naomi's advice. Still, this seemed like an extraordinarily bold thing to do.

Ruth anxiously watched until Boaz had fallen asleep. As she slipped up to him, she hesitated for a moment and listened for his even breathing. He

32

definitely was asleep, probably tired after such a long day of hard work. Ruth gently uncovered his feet and then lay down. How long, she wondered, would it take for him to grow cold enough to wake up? She felt so odd lying there waiting.

Just past midnight, Boaz stirred and then sat up. When he sensed someone at his feet, he asked in a startled voice, "Who are you? What are you doing here?"

"I'm Ruth, the young woman who has been gleaning in your fields these past weeks. Please," Ruth's voice faltered. But remembering Naomi's instructions, she gathered her courage and plunged forward with her little speech, "Please demonstrate that you will take care of me by covering me. If you are willing, you can do this because you are a near relative to my deceased husband."

Boaz hesitated for a moment. Ruth was significantly younger than he was. Could it be true that this young woman full of every godly quality a man could want in a wife was proposing that he should marry her? She obviously did mean that. There would be no other reason for her to be out in the middle of the night lying uncomfortably at his feet.

"Don't be afraid, Ruth," he comforted her. "I'll do exactly what you're asking me. Everyone knows your virtues. In the morning, I'll go make the arrangements. You need to know, though, there is a relative who is

even closer to you than I am. According to the law, he must be given the first opportunity to marry you."

So many times well-meaning Christians will say to me, "Just when I stopped looking, I met my spouse." I can't help but feel this is said with some piousness and the inference that if I would just accept my single state, God would automatically send me a husband. Almost without exception, these people were married in their early twenties. My mental response for the past several years has been, *Are you kidding me? You stopped looking when you hit twenty, miraculously met your spouse, dated for two years, and got married when you were twenty-two? You actually stopped looking when you turned twenty? I'd barely even started looking in earnest by then, but you'd already given up. Wow! You didn't have much endurance, did you?*

Other well-meaning people have told me, "If God wants you to meet someone, *He'll* bring that person to you." For many years I've struggled with this concept. Is it really a lack of faith or a sign of discontent to seek a husband? Does this concept of completely trusting God for everything really mean it is wrong to actively look for a spouse?

I believe trust in God is misapplied if it means you should sit idly by, waiting for something to happen. If people took that attitude, they could lose their jobs and believe God should magically give them new ones. Then those people could justify sitting at home and watching television until God dropped new jobs into their laps. The idea that we should sit around waiting for a job is so silly it hardly seems like it should be written down on paper. Finding a job takes work, and you have to be actively involved in that work. Most people update their resumes and send them out to potential employers. They fill out applications and look for job openings. Looking for a job is hard work, and almost no one gets a position without effort. Once in awhile things do just work out and a job comes to someone with very little effort, but that isn't how it normally happens.

When looking for a job, some people do seem to conquer the jobless situation much more easily than others. I, for instance, never have lacked for work. My particular set of skills is in high demand, and I happen to interview well. Other people who actually may have better skills may struggle more. They may be overqualified, they may not interview as well, or their highly-honed skills may be a fit only for very select jobs. In no way does this mean that the person is less worthy of a job than I am, but finding the perfect job fit may take longer for him or her.

I don't see much of a difference between looking for a job and looking for a spouse. Should one really expect to sit on the sidelines and think the right person will just happen by, look down, see you sitting there all lonely and by yourself, and choose you? Why would that person even notice you if you are on the sidelines and there is someone else who is equally charming and fun and actually in the game? Quite naturally, someone is drawn to look at the person who is doing something.

Each person is unique and brings special qualities to a relationship. Someone who may be very worthy of a spouse may find it more difficult to find the right person because he or she is, believe it or not, overqualified for most of the humdrum fish in the sea. A person may have very notable qualities that are stellar, but just as an engineer would not be a good fit for bagging groceries at the local supermarket, this person should not settle for Joe Average. He or she needs to find someone who compliments his or her special qualities. His or her spouse will have to be a very select and specific sort of person.

Regardless of how ridiculous the notion is that one should give up looking by the age of twenty or that it is wrong to keep looking for someone, there have been many times when I've felt guilty for not giving up but instead continuing on in my search. Well-meaning people have made me feel guilty because they make it seem like I'm unwilling to accept God's will for my life if I still desire to marry. Let me remind you that desiring a spouse is a very natural, God-given desire. He created Eve to be a helper for Adam. God's Word gives detailed instructions for marriage and relationships. To stifle that desire is to ignore something God has put in you.

I was encouraged when I realized that Ruth actually initiated a relationship with Boaz. On Naomi's suggestion, Ruth was the one who went to Boaz and made her desire for a relationship known. Now I'm still pretty much a traditionalist, so I will also rapidly remind you that once she made her intentions clear, she let Boaz do the pursuing. However, I think this is a clear example in the Bible where the woman did not sit around waiting for something to happen. She actively sought a husband.

Stepping it Up

So here you are. You don't feel called to be single, yet you are single. What steps are appropriate for you to take?

Step One: *Acknowledge that God's will for your life may include singleness and accept this possibility.*

This may seem confusing in light of the previous paragraphs, but it really doesn't need to be. If you sincerely believe in your heart that God has called you to be single, then you need to immerse yourself in what He has called you to be. God hasn't called anyone to be a no one, so if He truly means for you to be single, He must have something else very specific in mind for you.

I have met a few people who have felt called to a single life and the ministry they are allowed to have as a single person. They do not desire marriage and are incredibly happy in their singleness. When I've asked these people how they feel about marriage, they generally talk about the work God has them doing and how marriage might hamper that work. They have not been opposed to marriage but really believe God has kept them single for a purpose. Paul addresses this very issue in 1 Corinthians 7. He states that an unmarried person can focus on only the things of God; whereas, a married person must also take time to care for his or her family. In no way is caring for one's family wrong, but Paul understood the joy of literally pouring his life into spreading the gospel.

Step Two: *Do not let bitterness settle into your heart.*

Some people who deeply desire marriage are never given this gift. Why? I'm not sure we can fully know the answer to that, but I do know our purpose on earth is to glorify God. First Corinthians 10:31 says, "Therefore, whether you eat or drink, or whatever you do, do all to the glory of God." Oftentimes we can let bitterness over our circumstances keep us from glorifying God as we should.

Two people who had all the reason in the world to let their circumstances overwhelm them were Corrie and Betsie Ten Boom. They suffered horribly for the actions they took to protect Jews during World War II. Betsie perished in a concentration camp, and Corrie had to watch her sister slowly slip away from her. This was where God placed them. Through it all, they had peace; and through it all, God was glorified in a tremendous way. Many people, probably hundreds of them came to know Christ through the situation these sisters found themselves in, right in the middle of God's will. What a shame it would have been if Corrie and Betsie had bitterly withdrawn because they did not want to be there. The end result for their health and well being would not have changed, but their testimony certainly would have changed. All of those opportunities to share the love of God (the greatest purpose for them on earth) would have been lost.

In the midst of your heartache of singleness, protect your testimony. If singleness is where God has placed you, it is not wrong to look for a spouse, but do not let it override your testimony. Also, remember that the trials God allows in your life help you to grow into the person He wants you to be.

I experienced growth through trials firsthand when I was diagnosed with rheumatoid arthritis at the age of nineteen. I was in terrible pain, and I was afraid. My doctor told me that 5 percent of people diagnosed with the disease end up in wheelchairs within five years. When I look back on that time, I remember it as a terribly dark, discouraging, frightening, and painful time. That summer I had a mentally taxing job, and each evening I would come home from work and lie on the couch as the pain engulfed my body. Day after day I would come home, lie down, and cry.

One day I looked up and saw my mom quietly working about her tasks, trying not to disturb me. The realization of what it must be like to have a daughter come home every day and lie on the couch and cry horrified me. But I was hoping it wasn't coming across quite as badly as I thought, so I said, "I'm sorry, Mom. I guess I'm not very much fun to be around."

She said, "No, Honey. But we understand."

Ah! So it was that bad to be around me. I determined right then and there that no matter what, I was not going to come home and lie on the couch and cry even one more time; and I didn't.

For several years my body ached. I thought I was learning how to deal with and ignore the pain because the pain seemed to be lessening. Then a few years ago, I realized that I rarely ached anymore. I had a new physician and asked her about it. She ran some blood tests and told me my body did not have rheumatoid arthritis.

So what did I have? I don't know. Maybe God chose to heal me. Maybe I was misdiagnosed and had something entirely different. Why did God choose to remove that affliction from me? I probably will never know. What I do know is that on my own, I never would have chosen to go through those painful days, but I look back and see how much more sympathetic I am to ill people than I was prior to that experience. God also put two girls in my life during the time of my most intense pain who actually were crippled from the disease. I believe with all of my heart I was able to help them in a way others could not. What a shame it would have been if I had allowed bitterness and self pity to continue in my heart. I would have been unable to learn what God needed for me to learn and unable to minister to those two girls who needed my attention.

I've often heard preachers say that the happiest and safest place for a Christian is right in the middle of God's will. While being in God's will is the *best* place for us to be, it doesn't guarantee comfort and safety. Our purpose in life is to bring glory to God, and a willingness to allow God's perfect will in our lives may very likely bring some earthly trials. Look beyond the present, and rest in the joy that your obedience to God's will for your life will reap eternal benefits.

Step Three: *Work on your relationship with God.*

What is the one thing everyone says is key to a healthy marital relationship? Communication. In their relationship with God, what is one thing with which most Christians struggle? Communication. Keep on praying and talking to God. Keep on seeking what His next steps for your life are. Set aside time every day to pray.

Step Four: *Be the fun and happy person God created you to be.*

If you want someone to like you, you'd better like yourself. Be someone who is fun and likeable. Once in a while I'll walk away from a day and think,

Wow, I blew it today. I wouldn't expect anybody to like me; I didn't even like myself. Without fail, thoughts like these come on days when I allowed myself to react negatively to the circumstances around me.

Several days ago, the entire office was feeling grumpy because of a long string of dreary, overcast days. I heard the grumblings filtering into my office and decided to do something to lift the mood. I walked out to where several people were gathered and loudly announced, "I'm grossly offended by the weather today." Everyone laughed, including me. I enjoy laughing and making other people laugh too.

Step Five: *Dress attractively.*

I love to be comfortable, but I do not dress only for comfort. I'll never forget my sister coming to my house one day to "purge my closet of all evil." She started at one end of my closet, and as she worked her way through, she would occasionally pull things out and exclaim, "Please tell me you don't wear this anymore?" or "When did you last wear this?" or "This is too awful for even the thrift store." Finally, as she was nearing the end of my closet, she pulled out a drop waist denim jumper I loved. "Oh, Laura, what is *this* still doing in your closet?"

By that time, I'd had enough, and I said, "I love that jumper. I wear it all of the time, and I'm keeping it." We argued, but it was my dress and my closet. I kept it.

Two weeks later, I wore the unpopular jumper to work. When I got home, my neighbor girls were waiting on my doorstep to introduce their new teenage exchange student who would be living with them for the next three months. After the introductions, the exchange student looked at me, smiled, reached out, patted my tummy, and said, "When is your baby due?"

I did not have a protruding tummy, but the jumper suggested I should. I took that jumper off and got rid of it the next day. I called my sister and asked her to take me shopping. Since that time, I've made incredible strides in fashion, and my friends lovingly joke about me being a late bloomer. I wish I'd taken my sister's advice a few years earlier.

Step Six: *Accept invitations.*

Recently I was invited to the wedding of a friend I hadn't seen in quite a while. I debated and debated about whether or not to attend. Finally, I decided to go, and I had the best time. I ran into some other old friends, and we had a great visit during the reception. In addition, it was one more opportunity to meet new people (i.e. single guys). Four years after my brother's wedding, a guy who knew my sister-in-law and had noticed me at their wedding got up the courage to ask her about me—*four years later!* We actually went out several times.

Step Seven: *Be a friend to the friendless.*

When I was a kid and my family moved from the farm to the city, I think all of my brothers, my sister, and I felt a little out of place. Our family didn't have a lot of money, so we didn't have the most in-fashion clothes. I also felt overwhelmed by so many people everywhere. I never became popular in the cliquish sort of a way, but over time, all of my siblings and I became popular with what I like to call the common people. Our parents taught us to be kind to everyone regardless of what they looked like, their economic status, or how popular they were, and following their example, we were nice to everyone, even unpopular kids.

When I look back on my life, some of my best friends have been what I would have considered unlikely friendships. Opal was ninety-five when I turned twenty-seven. She used to call me when she was lonely, and I'd go over to her house (she still lived by herself). I really enjoyed her, and she taught me a lot about having a positive outlook on life. Then there was my neighbor who once told me her daughters lived by my comings and goings. Her girls used to come over to my house for cookies and crafts. I'm not saying these relationships are the same as a special someone, but having people in your life greatly reduces the ache of being alone.

Step Eight: *Develop interests and hobbies.*

Keeping a positive outlook on life is so much easier when you are busy. Don't allow yourself time to sit around and brood.

Recently I went to the library to check out some books and noticed a bluegrass band warming up in one of the bonus rooms. Instead of sitting at home wishing for something to do, I had a great time at a free concert.

Step Nine: *Keep current.*

I don't like this one. I actually hate listening to the news because it is so full of gloominess, but I've found that understanding what is going on in the world allows me to enter more freely and confidently into conversations.

Step Ten: *Be busy fulfilling God's purpose for your life, and be sincere in these endeavors.*

I recently began a Bible study with a brand new believer in Christ. Watching her learn and answering her questions gave me joy and purpose for myself that I previously had not understood.

I also began writing this book and working on other ministry-oriented projects. I found I couldn't stop thinking about Ruth. The more focused I became on this book, the more I looked forward to each day. I would find myself daydreaming about Ruth during meetings and wondering what a conversation with her would be like. I was jotting ideas and correlations on little scraps of paper and stuffing them into pockets and purses. All of that focus took me away from thinking about myself and gave me a drive to do something meaningful. Writing this book has been a tremendous learning experience for me. Studying the life of Ruth has reminded me of God's goodness and, although I may not understand it fully, His purpose for my life.

Your gifts and talents are different from mine, but they are no less special. God has a particular plan for you. Don't let your life be a waste. Do something that will count for eternity.

Step Eleven: *Surround yourself with fun people who also love God.*

These people, married or unmarried, will help you to maintain a good outlook on life. I often think of my friends Ryan and Stephanie. They are my best, non-relative, married friends. If ever there was an example of what a married couple should be to a single person, they are that example. Years ago, they started sitting with me in church. Occasionally, something will occur in church and we give each other those knowing looks. They are like a little extra family to me. They've done a lot of nice things for me and included me by having me over for dinner or taking me on fun excursions. Friendship is a two-way street, though. You cannot expect only to receive. I've had them over for dinner and tried to help them in ways that are unique to my abilities. To have friends, you must be a friend.

The steps above will not guarantee a husband for you, but they will guarantee a happy, more fulfilled life.

I keep looking for a husband because God created human beings to need companionship. If God doesn't have someone for me, I'll not grow bitter, but neither will I wonder if there was someone out there for me who I missed meeting because I never left my house. Whether or not that special someone exists, in the process of looking, I've met a group of people to whom I've ministered and many who have ministered to me.

CHAPTER 5

Does Not Now Mean Never?

*B*OAZ NORMALLY WOULD *have been overseeing the threshing, but instead, he was hurrying to the city gate. His mind was awhirl with thoughts. Who would have dreamed a few short weeks ago that he would be contemplating marriage today? He was glad he had been able to give Ruth extra grain from the threshing last night. Her life had been difficult, he knew that. Still, one would never know the sorrow she had experienced by the way she conducted herself.*

He wondered how long he would have to wait for Ruth's nearer relative to pass by the gate. Hopefully Boaz was early enough that he could catch the other relative before he headed out to do his own work. What if this nearer relative also wanted to marry

Ruth? "No," *Boaz firmly told himself,* "God meant Ruth for me. Providence placed her in my fields and then guided her to me last night. God's will shall be done."

Was that the relative? Boaz waited to be certain and then called out to him, "Come sit down, will you? I have some business I need to conduct with you. Wait, wait just a moment while I gather witnesses." *Boaz quickly called ten of the elders of the city over to him and waited for them to sit down before he began to talk.*

"A parcel of land that belonged to the widow Naomi's husband, Elimelech, needs to be purchased back for her. Naomi has no money or means by which to purchase back the land. If a kinsman-redeemer does not buy it for her, she'll have to wait until the Year of Jubilee before it will be given back to her family. As the nearest living relative, you have the honor of purchasing the piece of land for her. This is your opportunity to redeem it. If, however, you don't want to purchase the land, then I'll buy it." Boaz felt anxiety all over again. Of course this relative would want to buy it. To not redeem the property if it were within his means would almost be considered disgraceful.

"Really?" the relation seemed surprised. "I wasn't aware the land was for sale. But, yes, I'll definitely buy the land."

"You do realize," said Boaz, "that when you buy the land for Naomi you will also be buying it for Ruth the Moabitess. You will be obligated to marry her and raise up a child in the name of her dead husband."

Boaz watched as a slight frown appeared on the face of the man. "Oh, that does change things, doesn't it? I didn't realize there was a childless widow involved. I can't do it, Boaz. It would destroy my own inheritance. Go ahead. If you're willing to marry Ruth and raise children in Mahlon's name, go ahead and purchase the land. I relinquish my right to it." He reached down and quickly pulled the sandal from his foot and handed the shoe to Boaz. "In front of these witnesses, this sandal is a sign that I'm legally giving up the right to purchase the parcel of land."

With those final words from Ruth's nearest relative, Boaz knew the right to purchase the land and marry Ruth had been passed on to him. Even as Boaz was announcing to the witnesses that he did intend to redeem the land and marry Ruth, he felt relieved and suddenly very happy. Ruth would be his wife. He would care for her, and she would no longer be required to work long days in a field trying to gather enough food to feed herself and her mother-in-law.

Years ago, a good friend of mine asked my advice about whether or not she should marry a particular man. I knew she was getting ready to settle for second best, and I didn't want her to have less than what God wanted her to have. Knowing she feared that if she didn't take this offer she never would have another one, I asked her what it was she really wanted in a husband. What she described to me was nothing like the man she was considering. That, my friends, is the definition of settling. She was going to settle for much less than God's best, and believe me, it is tempting. I have been tempted from time to time because being alone is hard, and sometimes it seems it would be better to be with someone, even if that person isn't quite the right match, than to be all by yourself. When that temptation is strong, I remember the advice I gave to my friend: "Don't jump ahead of God. Wait for His plan in your life. As long as you're single, you can dream of the perfect spouse and what your relationship will be like." Of course, no man or woman is perfect, but while you are single, you are at liberty to look. You can date, and you can go out with friends when you want to do something fun. You can splurge and spend your grocery money on the perfect pair of shoes, and you won't have to explain to anyone why you can't afford to eat anything but popcorn and boxed macaroni for the following week.

A woman with the right partner wants to be with her husband. He is her best friend, and although she may not be able to splurge on the perfect shoes too often in exchange for a popcorn dinner, she will find contentment in a harmonious marriage. If, however, you don't have the right partner, you may wish you could date again, but you can't. You cannot go out with your friends anytime you want because you have responsibilities at home. Even when you are out with friends, you may feel awkward because you don't want them to guess that you don't have a good marriage. Your husband may even let you buy whatever you want, but new shoes won't fill the void of the love you crave. I've seen it too often. The loneliness of being without a spouse isn't even comparable to being married to the wrong person.

I told my friend to imagine that she is with a man she knows is not all God would want for her. Then after a few years of marriage, she runs into a single man who exactly fits her original description of what she wanted in a husband. He is godly, attractive, and finds her amusing; but of course he would never consider her because she is a married woman. I reminded her that as long as she was single, she could dream and look; but if she chose poorly, she wouldn't even have the solace of hoping one day to find a good husband.

Settle on God's Choice

The more I read the biblical account of Ruth, the more I identified with the choices Ruth faced. When Naomi told Ruth she had no more sons for her to marry, I believe they both thought that by staying with Naomi, Ruth was agreeing to be a widow and single woman for the rest of her life. First, Naomi implied that if Ruth were to stay in Moab, she might marry again: "And Naomi said to her two daughters-in-law, 'Go, return each to her mother's house. The Lord deal kindly with you, as you have dealt with the dead and with me. The Lord grant that you may find rest, each in the house of her husband....'" (Ruth 1:8–9a). Then Naomi implied that staying with her would mean they wouldn't marry again: "Turn back, my daughters, go—for I am too old to have a husband. If I should say I have hope, if I should have a husband tonight and should also bear sons, would you wait for them till they were grown? Would you restrain yourselves from having husbands? No, my daughters; for it grieves me very much for your sakes that the hand of the Lord has gone out against me!" (Ruth 1:12–13).

Ruth did not have any children to comfort her, and I am convinced she had no idea that God would provide a second husband for her. Any man who agreed to marry her would have to purchase back her father-in-law's property, and instead of that property going to his own sons, the property would be given to their son, who would bear the name of Ruth's dead husband. This meant the odds were really stacked against Ruth. She would have to marry someone who not only was attracted to her but also had significant means. If not already complicated enough, there were rules about who would be eligible to marry her. He would have to be a relative of her deceased husband, and if there were closer relatives, they would have the right to marry her first.

I can say with a certain degree of confidence that Boaz was an unexpected development for Ruth. Yet, her behavior before she met Boaz was completely unselfish. Not once do we see a hint of her feeling sorry for herself. In fact, when Boaz first meets Ruth, long before talk of marriage, he tells her everything she has done for Naomi is well known. "And Boaz answered and said to her, 'It has been fully reported to me, all that you have done for your mother-in-law since the death of your husband, and how you have left your father and your mother and the land of your birth, and have come to a people whom you did not know before'" (Ruth 2:11).

As I grow older, I often tell people I'm losing my physical beauty so now I need to start working on my personality. Of course, I'm just joking. But every person should work every day of his or her life on becoming more like Christ. By the comments Boaz made about Ruth, we know she portrayed an exemplary life, but Boaz was also a man with excellent character. In Ruth 2:1, the Bible states that Boaz was a man of great wealth, and one certainly can see he was a man of means. He owned his own fields and had the resources to become Ruth's kinsman-redeemer. However, the word translated *wealth* also can mean strength, ability, and efficiency. In other words, he was a man possessing the finest of qualities. Both Boaz and Ruth were people of integrity and worthy of each other.

In addition to working on my relationship with God and my spiritual character, I work at staying in shape, keep my wardrobe up-to-date, try to stay up on current events, and maintain good healthy relationships with friends and family. (It's good practice for that really great relationship I'm looking forward to some day.) I do all of these things because I'm a firm believer that just because God hasn't given me a husband right now does not mean He won't give me one in the future. In the meantime, I do a fair amount of dreaming and looking. Remember, God is a God of miracles. No matter how impossible you think your situation is,

God can provide in ways we could never imagine. He did for Ruth.

Do you ever try to think up all the ways God could work things out? I saw a cartoon once in which a man was kneeling beside his bed with his head bowed in prayer. The caption said something like this, "OK God, here's my plan." I'll be honest; I've been guilty more than a few times of laying out *my* plan for God to follow.

Remember the miracles that are recorded for us in the Bible. Do you think that when Jesus performed His first miracle, Mary, His mother, had any idea how He would provide more wine for the wedding feast? Do you think she knew what He was going to do when she told the servants to seek Jesus' assistance? If I'd been her, I would have been trying to figure out where He could buy more wine, or I would have imagined some guests showing up late to the wedding with gifts of wine, but I never would have dreamed that He would just turn water into wine.

I frequently pray for my miracle (a husband), and I know that if God decides to perform that miracle for me, it won't be like drinking watered-down grape juice. He will provide just the right man for me, and it will be exactly in His timing.

Now is the time for us to grow into the people God wants us to be. When this time has passed and if marriage never came, we'll already be in heaven, and then it will either all make sense or we will no longer care. I like to think that it will make sense and we will see how our lives and circumstances were tailored to touch other people.

CHAPTER 6

Why Don't I Get to Be a Mother?

NAOMI KNEW THAT she shouldn't be tired; Ruth had done all of the hard work. Yet as she cradled baby Obed in her arms and smiled at Ruth and Boaz, she felt exhausted from overseeing the birth of her first grandchild. Was it possible to have so much joy? Had she ever doubted God's goodness? There was so much she'd learned from Ruth, this woman who was many years younger than she was. How precious Ruth was to her. What was it the women in Bethlehem said about her? They said that she, this Ruth who loved Naomi, was better to Naomi than seven sons.

Even then Naomi could not know the extent of God's goodness to her. Her daughter-in-law Ruth had become, with the birth of Obed, the great-grandmother of the future king of Israel, Kind David. He would be *known as one of Israel's most important kings, the man after God's own heart.*

I'm not sure there is anything more emotionally painful than to desperately want children but be unable to have them. Married or unmarried, the tears that have been spent on this are nearly immeasurable.

Mother's Day is perhaps the most excruciating day of the year for women who are childless. I often contemplated staying home from church but always ended up with some responsibility that left me sitting in the pew fighting tears. Laughter and tears have a lot in common. When it is most socially unacceptable, they tend to make an unsightly appearance. Anyone who has ever gotten the giggles in church or, on the opposite end of the emotional spectrum, been tempted to cry at work, can understand the horror of these emotions.

For years I thought it was my own lack of maturity that caused me to want to skip Mother's Day. I was wracked with guilt because I truly was thankful for my own mother, grandmothers, and the mothers to my nieces and nephew. So how could I be so self-centered and think of my own situation when I should be honoring them?

I well remember the worst Mother's Day of my life. Looking back on it now, it takes on an almost comical air; however, at the time, it was anything but. The service began with the pastor asking all of the mothers to come line up in front of the auditorium. The pews emptied out as the women made their way up to the front and semi-circled around, wrapping halfway down the side aisles. From my vantage point, I couldn't see one other grown woman besides myself still seated. I felt completely conspicuous. What I could see in addition to good mothers were neglectful mothers, unwed mothers, and teenage mothers all standing in front of me while the pastor droned on and on about how these women were the ones who would make a difference in the world. Everything that would ever be invented, built, written, or accomplished from here on out would be a direct result of these most amazing women. Mothers had all of the influence. Each woman then took a turn naming her offspring. At long last, I gratefully closed my eyes for the long, flowery prayer that ensued. As the mothers traipsed back to their seats, I breathed a sigh of relief. I had been able to quickly wipe away the one tear that had stubbornly fought its way out of my eyes.

But we were not done; the pastor remembered that he had flowers to pass out to all of the mothers. I watched while the women in front of me and on either side of me accepted their flowers. *Please, God, let this end before I start crying!* Finally, the ushers finished up at the back of the auditorium. Then suddenly someone remembered there was baby's breath to go with the carnations. Once again, I watched while the women in front of me and on either side of me accepted their baby's breath and murmured their happiness.

I cried all the way home. Thankfully, it would be another year before I had to go through this again, or so I thought. During the evening service, the pastor remembered yet one more special Mother's Day surprise—books they'd forgotten to pass out in the morning. One final time, I watched the women in front of me and the women on either side of me accept their books. The usher extended a book to me, and just as I began to reach for it, he pulled his hand back. I heard him mutter, "Oops." I could feel the red creeping up the back of my neck and completely encompassing me. I wanted to die.

One day, I decided to interview friends and acquaintances who either were single or who never had been able to have children. I specifically chose women who expressed joy for other mothers. I wanted to know why I seemingly was the only one who struggled so much. I even spoke to women who'd had miscarriages and had never been able to carry a baby to full term. The topic was sensitive, so I began by explaining the difficult time I had with Mother's Day and my longing for a child.

As I spoke with these women, I asked specifically about Mother's Day, and I was surprised to find that Mother's Day was a nightmare for countless women. Some finally had come to the point of skipping the Mother's Day worship service because it had become too painful to endure. As they told me their stories, I could completely identify. Many of the same things had happened to me. Many of the same careless statements had been made to me: "At least you don't have to put up with kids who will break your heart," or "I'd give anything to have free time like you do," or "I wish I could get a vacation from my kids," or "Are you a mother? These carnations are only for the mothers," or "Bet you wish you had one of these babies," or "You couldn't know how hard it is to be a mother." I also was not the only one who had been offered a gift on Mother's Day only to have it snatched back. Knowing how hard it had been for me, I could only imagine how much more difficult it would be for someone who actually had lost a baby or babies.

Like me, these women suffered tremendous guilt because they knew they should be thankful for the many blessings they did have. But the pain, the endless pain of not having a child made Mother's Day a wretched event. Most of them had never expressed the hurt they felt on Mother's Day because they didn't want to be viewed as bitter.

God eventually blessed a couple of my childless friends with children. These friends now often call me on or around Mother's Day to let me know they are praying for me. They remember how very difficult the day was before they had children. I can't begin to describe what a blessing their prayers and phone calls are to me.

My own siblings have made a particular effort to educate their children in loving their auntie. With a little prompting from their moms and dads, these special children in my life call me when they are excited about their own accomplishments or to congratulate me when I have achieved some success. One of my sisters-in-law will often show up at my work with my nieces on my birthday to make it an extra special day. If you're married and have the opportunity to touch a single or childless person's life this way, do not neglect your opportunity to share your children.

I wish I could say I've completely conquered my disappointment over my childlessness. I'm not sure, however, that is what God has in mind. God's perfect plan was for Adam and Eve to be fruitful and multiply. Sin came into our world and made it an imperfect place, a place where some women are barren and others do not find a mate. Even though we may be disappointed, God still has expectations of us in this imperfect world. We have a responsibility to do our part in nurturing and loving other human beings, including children. God does not want us to live in bitterness. Below I have listed a few things that have helped me immensely when it comes to dealing with this part of my life.

1. *Realize you are not alone in this sorrow.* I have often thought of Hannah in the Bible and how she suffered not just from careless remarks but from mean-spirited comments from her husband's second wife.

2. *Reach out to someone else who is childless.* Don't do this to discuss your childlessness but instead to let that person know how meaningful she is in your life. I call my favorite single aunt, and we laugh and talk about things she did with/for me and catch up on life. I think about what she has meant to me and know it is a fallacy to think I don't matter to other people.

3. *Ask your friends to pray for you*—especially the ones who you know care. Do *not* ask friends who have made insensitive comments to you in the past. They are likely to repeat the mistake, not because they are mean people but because they do not fully understand or are not empathetic by nature. Talking your situation over with them may be setting yourself up for further pain.

4. *Know God cares.* He really cares about this heartache of yours. He created you and knows you better than you know yourself. Remember our role on earth is to glorify God. Being bitter will not give you a baby, but bitterness will ruin your life and destroy your testimony.

5. *Do not go to church or another event where you know you may struggle when you are tired!* Be rested. I'll occasionally say, "I'm so tired, I could cry." Tears and weariness go hand in hand, so don't set yourself up to have a breakdown.

6. *Read your Bible and pray specifically about how you're feeling when you know you're going to be in one of those emotionally charged situations.*

7. *Show your pastor this chapter.*

If you're a pastor and reading this, you might be thinking, *Whoa, this is a landmine! I'm not going to ignore Mother's Day because there are a few women who will feel bad, but I don't want to hurt anyone either.* May I share with you that those of us who do not have children never would want you to stop honoring mothers on Mother's Day. Those mothers are pretty important to us too.

I have been in churches where Mother's Day was handled so tactfully that I was not left with the agonizing feelings previously described. A few years ago, I attended a church in Tennessee, and the pastor handled the day so beautifully that I felt only gratitude for my mother and the role I play as a woman. The pastor asked the typical Mother's Day questions: (1) Who's the oldest mother? (2) Who's the mother with the most children? (3) Which mother traveled the furthest to be here? (4) Who's the newest mother, etc. He then asked the mothers to stand in their places, and he prayed for them.

After the prayer, the pastor talked about godly women. "Some women will never biologically bear children, or for that matter, have a child who calls them mother," he said. He went on to talk about how these women can vastly impact children's lives (Sunday school teachers, aunts, and women in the church who take an interest in children). He talked about how all women can and should have a positive effect on children's lives. Then he preached his sermon, which included a challenge to mothers and all women to be godly examples. As we left the service, teenage girls stood at the door passing out the typical Mother's Day favors. They did not ask anyone if she was a mother; they simply handed *all* women the pretty bookmark, smiled, and said, "Happy Mother's Day." You know, that was a happy Mother's Day for me. I still missed having a baby to hold, my own child to hug and kiss, but I did not feel like a leftover.

Speaking of leftovers, at all costs, avoid waiting until the end of the day to give leftover Mother's Day gifts to the single or barren women. When this happens to me, I remind myself that I am not a leftover woman and the intentions are good. That helps, but it would be much better if all women received the Mother's Day token gift at the same time.

I Only Needed to Ask

I hesitate to write this because to me it is extremely personal. I wonder what people will think of me to know this ever went on in my head; yet, as I've talked to others, I've found that they've experienced this same emotion. This powerful emotion has the potential to rob you of one of the greatest joys you can experience. Be cautious, just because I confess it to you and tell you it is a natural reaction, do not allow yourself for a moment to think it is correct. The reaction is natural because we are sinners, but God can completely and swiftly remove it from your heart. For me, this feeling lasted a very short time, probably less than five minutes at a time, but I've experienced it more than once. Each time I've prayed the same prayer, and each time I've been blessed beyond what I ever could hope.

With clarity, I remember the first time I was told that I was going to be an aunt. As I write this, I literally have tears in my eyes and feel a huge lump in my throat. I love each of my nieces and my nephew fiercely. I cannot imagine life without each and every one of them. Yet, the emotions I experienced as I was told I was going to be an aunt were a mixture of pain, joy, and jealousy. My instant thought was, *God, don't you know how much I want to be a mother? I've always wanted to be a mother. I want to be a mother more than anyone I know. I'm getting so old. Are you never going to let me be a mother? Why does she get blessed with a child and not me?* This cry is almost verbatim to what went through my head as I smiled, hugged, and congratulated my sister-in-law. I was fighting tears and struggling to smile at the same time. Yet, even at that moment, I was excited and happy that I would be an aunt.

If you have never experienced two such fiercely competing emotions, you must take my word for the completely confusing situation that it is.

I am thankful that God spoke to my heart the very first time I ever experienced this, and I immediately followed that first prayer with a second. *Dear God, thank you that I'm going to be an aunt. Please don't let me ruin this wonderful thing with jealousy. Help me to be only excited and happy.* From that moment on, I was filled with a wonderful and pure joy. I believe I am a *special* aunt to all three of my nieces and my one nephew. However, I easily could have missed out on all of the joy by letting bitterness creep into my life because I did not have my very own baby.

I have also prayed that God would not let me feel jealousy regarding friends and acquaintances who are expecting. God has also given me victory in this area, and all I had to do was ask Him for it. When my friends tell me they're expecting, I feel genuinely thrilled for them. Again, you are the one who will suffer the most if you allow bitterness into your life. And jealousy is an acid that will burn your heart away.

Baby Obed

One of the biggest pitfalls a single person can fall into is dreading the future. The future so rarely turns out to be what we expect it to be, but we often try to predict the future based on our immediate circumstances. How many people have you known who have retired expecting to travel and enjoy a long retirement only to discover they have a terminal illness and then die almost immediately? How many people have you known who have been given a very scary cancer diagnosis, but ten to fifteen years later, are still living a strong and meaningful life?

I've often worried about the future. I've wondered what it will be like when all of my friends are grandmas and I'm just an old maid. My thoughts once again turn to the story of Ruth. Naomi urged her two daughters-in-law to return to their homelands and families. She said, "Turn back, my daughters, go—for I am too old to have a husband. If I should say I have hope, if I should have a husband tonight and should also bear sons, would you wait for them till they were grown? Would you restrain yourselves from having husbands? No, my daughters; for it grieves me very much for your sakes that the hand of the LORD has gone out against me!" (Ruth 1:12–13).

Poor Naomi. She was without hope. How sad that she let her grief remove all hope of fulfillment and happiness from her life. She had stopped trusting God for her future. To be perfectly honest, most of us would react in a similar fashion. She was without means, a husband, or children. The future certainly must have seemed very grim. Perhaps she also worried about growing old without grandchildren, and who could blame her? To be childless during that time was viewed as a curse.

Yet Naomi was not destined to live in this situation for long. In a short time, her daughter-in-law met and married a wealthy man. Because of the customs of the nation of Israel, the firstborn son to this new union was by law Naomi's grandson. Baby Obed was born to Ruth and Boaz, and the Bible says that Naomi became a nurse to the baby boy. Naomi's circumstances changed overnight.

The women of the community certainly viewed Naomi as a blessed woman. They said, "...blessed be the Lord, who has not left you this day without a close relative; and may his name be famous in Israel!" (Ruth 4:14).

Do you realize how famous that name has become? Baby Obed was the grandfather of David. Jesus is a direct descendant of David. Do you remember in the beginning of this book when we talked about how important Ruth's role in God's plan was? Ruth, a Gentile, was part of Jesus' lineage. Don't ever for a moment believe that you cannot be part of God's plan.

Let me encourage you that the circumstances of your life today do not have to determine your future. I cannot promise that you will find someone to marry or that you will have children. I cannot promise you grandchildren. I can, however, promise you that if you live each day in the center of God's will, He will give you peace and joy. I also can promise that you will experience blessings along the way that you never expected or would be able to predict.

CHAPTER 7

Why I'll Never Be Alone

*T*WO WEARY WOMEN *had traveled to Bethlehem, and God miraculously provided a husband and a son.*

Many years later, two more weary travelers would enter Bethlehem, and another son would be born—the Son of God, the Savior of the world. "For unto us a Child is born, Unto us a Son is given; And the government will be upon His shoulder. And His name will be called Wonderful, Counselor, Mighty God, Everlasting Father, Prince of Peace" (Isa. 9:6).

"Why I'll Never Be Alone" isn't a question; it's a statement. Please do not skip this chapter because it is the most important chapter of all.

One of the biggest struggles of singleness is the notion that a single person is alone. I remember one of my married girlfriends calling me up once to see if I would go to a graduation with her. Her husband was out of town, and she didn't want to go by herself. Her exact words were, "I hate going to things like this by myself. You're used to going to things by yourself, so it doesn't bother you."

In a way, she was right. I have, for the most part, become used to attending functions by myself. I still would rather have someone go with me, but it's not the social functions that are hard. The evenings and nighttimes are the hardest of all.

I will never forget the night I was awakened around 1:00 AM by a loud thud inside my house that was followed by an ear-piercing yowl from my cat, Mercedes. I didn't need to see it to know what it was. The thud sounded exactly like a body hitting the floor, and I knew someone was in my house and had just tripped over Mercedes. The sound came from the dining room, just down the hall from my bedroom.

I sat bolt upright in bed. My heart was pounding so hard I could barely breathe. My hand slid over to the other side of my bed and grasped the handgun my dad had given me. Trembling, I sat in bed, staring at the bedroom door. I knew I didn't have time to call 911. This was a situation I was going to have to deal with by myself. I felt like I was going to vomit, but I swallowed hard. I had to stay in control. *Please God, please, please God, help me.* Suddenly I felt calm, and then it happened again. This horrible person had tripped on my cat and again fallen to the floor. Mercedes yowled like she'd been terribly injured. Strength and calmness filled me in an amazing way. I was not going to sit there and let some man come down the hall and rape or murder me. I decided in a flash that I'd get him while he was still down on the floor. I leapt out of bed and ran down the hall. My mind was alert, my body was nimble, and the fear was in control.

When I reached the dining room, Mercedes' back was arched, and all of her fur stood on end; but she wasn't looking at a body in the middle of the room or even at me. She was staring at the sliding glass door. With my heart pounding, I looked too. Just as my eyes turned to the glass, something hit it with a terrific thud, which was immediately followed by another yowl from Mercedes. My heart seemed to stop ever so briefly. I then realized the cause of the thud was a very furious black cat. She wanted to fight with Mercedes but couldn't get to her.

Have you ever had a sense of relief so great that it left you weak, so weak you almost no longer could stand? All of a sudden, my strength was gone. I wobbled over to a dining room chair and sank down onto it. I waited while my heart slowly returned to a normal rate. After a time, I became aware that I was chilly, and I knew then that my senses were returning. Over and over in my head I kept saying, *Thank you, God, thank you!*

Later, when I looked back on the unfolding of those events, I realized my strength came when I called out to God. The fact that the noise turned out to be two cats fighting rather than an intruder did not change the fear I had experienced.

Even nonreligious people call out to God in times of distress or fear. Have you ever asked yourself why? Could it be that each of us knows deep in our hearts that there must be One greater than ourselves, but only in a moment of great need do we turn towards and call out to that One? What a shame that we wait until that moment of panic to call on God, because He is right there for us every moment of every day.

I recently spoke to a single friend of mine who had just come to know God. She and I were talking about how different her life was from mine. I had been raised in a family where I was taught about God from the time I was a small child. When I was very young, I accepted Him as my Savior. She had only recently taken this step of faith. In her words, let me describe her experience:

All of my life I've had fear, and it has been like an elastic band around my heart. I feared I would lose my job and wouldn't be able to pay my rent. I feared I would make someone angry or that someone was gossiping about me. I feared what people thought of me or how I would react if a disaster occurred. I wondered what would happen if I fell down the stairs. How long would it take someone to find me? The fear was always there, sometimes small and sometimes big; but it was always there, pressing against my heart. Then I accepted Christ as my Savior, and suddenly the elastic band around my heart was gone. I cannot tell you what freedom it is to know that God is always there, and He is always with me. I know it doesn't mean nothing bad will ever happen to me, but I no longer have to go through things alone.

She was right. Life is full of lots of little fears and moments of aloneness. Experiences such as the raw fear of an intruder are relatively few, but how do we deal with those day-to-day moments of aloneness?

Let God Become Your Protector

Think one final time of our story of Ruth. When she returned to Bethlehem with Naomi, she stated, "…your people shall be my people, And your God, my God" (Ruth 1:16). Ruth had made a conscious and personal decision to turn away from the false gods of her youth and walk with God. This decision was not one Naomi could make for her. Ruth had to make it for herself, and how amazing that the Creator of the universe accepted her, a woman who wasn't even one of God's chosen people of the race of Israel.

Later, Ruth gleaned in Boaz's field and Boaz took notice of her and provided for her. She asked him why, and he said, "The LORD repay you for your work, and a full reward be given you by the LORD God of Israel, under whose wings you have come for refuge" (Ruth 2:12). The idea of being under God's wings is the same as a mother hen gathering her chicks under her wings for protection.

Another reason God calls on us to walk with Him is so He can fill us with the peace and comfort only He can give. He wants to gather us under His wings as His children so He can protect and care for us. To take advantage of the wonderful peace only God can give, you also must take that personal and conscious step of faith.

The Bible tells us in Romans 3:23 that we are all sinners. The Bible does not mince words on this subject. It says, "For all have sinned and fall short of the glory of God." This verse is telling us that we are not good enough in and of ourselves. Furthermore, in Romans 6:23 it says, "For the wages of sin is death…" The price of our sin is death or eternal separation from God. So how does this fit in with a God who wants to cover me with His wings and protect me? It fits because that verse does not stop with the death part. The verse goes on to say, "…but the gift of God is eternal life in Christ Jesus our Lord."

Almost everyone has heard John 3:16 quoted to them. But without understanding why we need a gift, it probably never has made sense. Let me give you that verse now in the context of why we need a gift: "For God so loved the world [the world is sinful, including you and me] that He gave His only begotten Son [that Son is sinless Jesus Christ] that whoever [that's you and me again] believes in Him should not perish [*perish* means death or eternal separation from God] but have everlasting life [life that is not separated from God]."

Is it really that simple? All I have to do is turn from my sin and believe? Yes! It is that simple. Romans 10:9–10, 13 says, "That if you confess with your mouth the Lord Jesus and believe in your heart that God has raised Him from the dead, you will be saved. For with the heart one believes unto righteousness, and with the mouth confession is made unto salvation….For whoever calls on the name of the Lord shall be saved."

But shouldn't I have to do something besides believe? The Bible is clear about this matter as well. Ephesians 2:8–9 says, "For by grace you have been saved through faith, and that not of yourselves; it is the gift of God, not of works, lest anyone should boast." In other words, you can't save yourself and you can't take the credit. Only God has the power to save you. He completed the work when He sent His Son to die for your sinfulness. Our own good works cannot buy a right standing with God.

You may be thinking, *Yes, but is this really the same God who promised to protect Ruth?*

With confidence, I can say, "Yes!" because Christ so perfectly fulfilled the prophecies of the Old Testament. Isaiah recorded seven hundred years before Jesus was born that a child would be born of a virgin. Isaiah 7:14 states, "Therefore the Lord Himself will give you a sign: Behold, the virgin shall conceive and bear a Son, and shall call His name Immanuel." Micah also prophesied that this ruler would come from Bethlehem. Micah 5:2 says, "But you, Bethlehem Ephrathah, though you are little among the thousands of Judah, yet out of you shall come forth to Me the One to be ruler in Israel, whose goings forth are from of old, from everlasting."

How precious that God used Ruth, obedient in her singleness, and Bethlehem, a seemingly insignificant place, to complete His perfect plan. The God of Ruth's day is the same God who will cover the single, the widowed, the married, the old, and the young with His wings.

A God who loves you enough to send His Son to die for you does not look at a single person as an incomplete leftover. When you are one of God's own, you are a complete, whole person. You are a person He wants to use to further His plan. Let Him use you!

> ...you are complete in Him...
>
> —Colossians 2:10a

LaVergne, TN USA
12 January 2011
212214LV00001B/1/P